The Journey

Steph Loughman

© 2016 Steph Loughman
All rights reserved.

ISBN: 1532707940
ISBN 13: 9781532707940
Library of Congress Control Number: 2016906306
CreateSpace Independent Publishing Platform
North Charleston, South Carolina

This book is dedicated to all children whose lives were ended far too soon because of the lie of abortion—including my own child, Joshua Daniel—and to all the mothers who weep silent tears of remorse, guilt, and shame.

Contents

Preface		vii
Joshua's Journey		1
Chapter One	All Good Things Must Come to an End	3
Chapter Two	A New Home	9
Chapter Three	Problems Outside of Paradise	13
Chapter Four	What a Dream!	17
Chapter Five	A New Friend	24
Chapter Six	A Praise Session	30
Chapter Seven	Family Ties	36
Mommy's Journey		43
Chapter One	My Changing World	45
Chapter Two	The Procedure	49
Chapter Three	A New Life	53
Chapter Four	Take It to the Cross	59
Chapter Five	A Wonderful Dream	65
Chapter Six	Friends and Forgiveness	70
Chapter Seven	A Purpose for Joshua and Sierra	78
A Message for You		85

Preface

My life began very simply—just like any other life. Every person's existence begins in one moment. While the circumstances may vary in every situation, all life starts the same. However, when you really think about it, nothing about the way someone's life comes about is important. The significant information is all of the events that happen afterward. What the person felt, how he or she loved, and who loved him or her—these are the important things. These are the key factors that we can take from a person's life and enable an individual's existence to extend long past his or her short—sometimes extremely short—time on earth.

Thus, my life began just as any other life begins. My mommy found out she was pregnant. All of the normal emotions were present in her; she was scared, happy, and nervous. She felt the whole mixture of the good and bad feelings that can be associated with a positive pregnancy test. I know she felt these emotions because I could feel them all. Mommy and I were connected, both literally and figuratively. As I grew inside of her body, I felt every single thing that she felt. Nervous, scared, happy, shaken—whatever the emotion might be, it took a toll on her body, which in turn had an effect on my body as well.

Now, obviously I wouldn't have understood this at the time, but my mommy was under a lot of pressure. She was living in a very bad situation, and there were many scary things in her life. I am not sure that I even completely understand these hard things now, but that is OK because I really don't have to. Sometimes, after time has gone by and things have happened, the reasons don't really matter anymore. But things were about to change for her in ways that she could not even imagine! Things were going to go from hopeless to terrible to amazing!

Joshua's Journey

Chapter One

All Good Things Must Come to an End

My story should probably start with introductions of my family. I never really got the chance to get to know a lot of my family, but I always heard my mommy talking about how she had a lot of family. She talked like she really loved them and loved being close to them. To be honest, I was excited to get to know them. Aunts, uncles, cousins, grandmas, and grandpas—I had them all! They never got to meet me, but I bet they would've loved me. I like to think that we will all get to know each other quite well one day. I can't wait to be introduced to them; it will be the best family reunion *ever*!

The family that I did know consisted of a brother, a sister, and my parents. My brother was just a baby when I was in our mommy's belly, so he never really got to know much about me. I know he would have loved me if we had gotten the chance to meet. We would have had a lot of fun playing with each other and growing up together! I also had a sister, and she was a teenager. She was so excited to meet me. I heard her asking my mommy about me all of the time. She would ask my mommy how she was feeling and would ask a lot of questions about me and how I was growing in her belly. I'm sure that my sister was excited to meet me.

Then there was the man whom I was supposed to call my daddy; he was not a nice man. I had noticed that my mommy was always upset when he was around. There was not a lot of peace around him; instead, he caused a lot of fighting and unhappiness. Mommy and I usually felt fear when Daddy was around. I never felt safe in his presence. I don't think my mommy did either. One day, I remember hearing my mommy tell him that he needed to go away and not come back. How I hoped that he would so that we could be happy! I didn't like being afraid, and I didn't like the feeling that I would get when my mommy was afraid.

Then there's my mommy. Of course, I'm closest to her. I lived in her belly! Oh, it was so comfortable there. I loved it when she would rub her belly and talk to me! I heard her sing to me and tell me she loved me. I felt everything that she felt. When she was happy, I was too; when she was sad, I was too. Can you be any closer to another person as a baby? I can't think of any way. I wish I had gotten more time with her. I am positive that one day I will get to see her again. I know that she will know me and that I definitely will know her. Even with the distance between us now, our bond will never be fully broken. I think remembering our bond might help us both deal with the separation that we have right now.

The Journey

That's it for the family introductions. They were all I knew. Maybe I can tell you more about all of my family after we get to have our amazing reunion. But for now, we will move on to that day—that fateful day that would change not only my life but also the lives of my family forever.

♦ ♦ ♦

I remember being all snuggled up in my mommy's belly one morning and having this feeling that something was wrong. I could feel Mommy's heart beating in a different way than normal. She was scared again, but this time, it was a different fear than when my dad was around. She was rubbing her belly, and she kept saying, "I'm sorry. I have no other choice." I wondered who she was talking to and why she was crying so much. I wish there was a way that I could have comforted her! I wanted to let her know that I loved her so much and that it made me sad to feel how sad she was.

The only way that I could think of to make her feel better was to move around and remind her that I was there. But this time, when I moved, she felt it! Oh, I thought she would be so happy to feel me move! I know that she felt me move because every time I would turn around in her belly, I would feel her grab her stomach. Once I heard her say this: "Oh my goodness, I felt the baby move!" I thought that she would be happy, but there was sadness in her voice. Didn't she want to feel me move?

She was on her way to the doctor, but she kept moving around like she couldn't get comfortable. I felt her heart racing, and she had the most incredible sadness that any person has ever known. I felt the tears that she was trying so hard to keep deep inside of her. I still didn't know why she was so sad, but it made me want to cry. I could tell that she was crying almost constantly. When we got to the doctor's office, I heard the doctor ask her if she wanted to see the ultrasound. Yay! Mommy was going to get to see another picture of me! I knew she loved to do that; I heard her talking to the picture of me that she had from before.

But she told the doctor that she did *not* want to see my new picture. I remember thinking to myself, "Why not, Mommy? I promise that I'll smile real big for you!" I knew something was dreadfully wrong. I tried to hear what the doctor was saying. I thought to myself, "Why isn't my mommy running out of the room screaming?" I moved around like crazy to remind her that I was there. I wanted her to remember that she didn't need to be afraid because I was there and because we would be all right. She seemed to get sadder with every move I made. I didn't understand why she didn't want to feel me move. Didn't she know how much I loved her? That day was just not right, and I felt things were going to get very bad. I just couldn't comprehend why.

Things calmed down a bit, and we left the doctor's office. I thought we were out of the woods. Whatever was wrong was clearly something that I couldn't see, but maybe now she would feel better. I didn't understand that the road we were

The Journey

starting down had no happy ending. We were going home, so I thought things must be OK. Boy, I was wrong! Mommy was very tense that night. I tried like before to make her happy; I rolled and rolled around in her belly to let her know how much I loved her and how comfortable her belly was for me. I did not realize that this would be the last night that I would be all snuggled up in my mommy's womb.

◆ ◆ ◆

The next day, I felt even more sadness. Mommy's belly was doing funny things, and everything felt weird. I just knew something wasn't right, but I didn't know what was wrong. We were going to the hospital. I heard someone say this: "You need to go to the labor and delivery department." I thought this: "Wait, that can't be right!" I knew I still had so much more growing to do. There was no way I was ready to come into the world. I needed to stay in Mommy's belly a little longer. I tossed and turned. I was moving all over the place, but it seemed that every time I moved, it made Mommy even sadder. She was crying continually. What was going on? If I could have spoken, the only words I would've said are these: "Mommy, I love you!" I would have said those words over and over again. But things were quickly fading away.

I felt things in Mommy's body moving all around, and then I felt pain. I wasn't quite sure what I was feeling, but I knew that it hurt. But then I saw a light—something that I had never seen before. It wasn't like a light in a room; it was a person! I wondered, "Who was this man who is more beautiful than words can explain?" Then He told me that His name was Jesus. He told me to focus on Him rather than the pain. He talked to me, and He held me; He told me that He loved me and that things would be all right. Jesus said that He was going to take me to live with Him and that I would see my mommy again one day at His house.

Then I looked at my mommy. I had been inside her for a long time and felt her feelings, but I had never seen her. She was asleep, but I was so glad that I got to see her face. Even though confusion, fear, and regret were clearly written on her face, she was so pretty. I'm sure that she didn't hear me, but Jesus told me that I could tell her good-bye. I remember that He held me close to her face, and I remember that I whispered this: "Good-bye, Mommy. I love you so much. I don't understand what just happened here, but I will miss you so much, and I can't wait until I will see you again." Then Jesus took me to His home.

Chapter Two

A New Home

All of the things from before seemed to fade away. I had already forgotten about all the pain from before because I was so comfortable and happy with Jesus. He held me so tightly and lovingly that I felt so secure and peaceful that nothing else mattered. When Jesus and I got to heaven, I couldn't believe how beautiful it was! Words really can't describe the beauty of that new home, but I will try to help you comprehend the majesty of heaven. I will explain how I saw it and how I still experience Jesus and heaven.

When I first arrived, the best thing about heaven was Jesus. He was and still is more amazing than anyone could ever imagine! There was such love in His eyes that it made me shiver to think about His love. When He looked at me, I knew that I was in the best place ever and that nothing could be better than heaven. Now Jesus and I talk often; He really is my best friend! He reminds me all the time that my mommy didn't mean to do what she did, and He tells me that she still loves me very much. He knows her just like He knows me, so He knows how she really felt that day and still feels now.

There are other beings here. They are called "angels." Oh, they are so beautiful! They do not all look the same. Just like people, they all have an individual look, but they are all amazingly magnificent. The best thing about the angels is that they always give praise to God. The angels are always singing praises to God; that's all that they do. They talk and sing about how marvelous He is.

There are all of the people who believed in Jesus and asked Him to forgive their sins when they were alive. There are people just like me in heaven too. There are people whose lives on earth ended before they were old enough to ask for forgiveness, and they all got to come live here too. We get to live here forever and praise God for all of eternity! It's so exciting to know that. Everyone is so happy here. There is no pain, sadness, or regret here. There is only joy and love.

There's something else that is special about the people here in heaven. Some of them are my family members! Not long after I got to heaven, Jesus introduced me to someone very special—my great-grandma! She died just ten short days after I did, but time is different in heaven than it is on earth, so waiting for her to get there was like no time at all. My mommy was very close to her grandma, and Jesus told me that Momaw was very excited to meet me. When Momaw (that's what I call her) saw me, she started running to meet me! She said it was wonderful to be introduced to her great-grandson! She said I looked a lot like my mommy too, and that was very special for me to hear. We talked and talked. It was so nice to hear more about my mommy. Momaw and I have a lot of special times together now. We are both very excited to see my mommy again one day.

One thing that Momaw explained to me helped me understand a little bit about who I am also. You see, there is a gorgeous river here in heaven. I have always felt kind of drawn to the river, and I love to just sit and stare at the water. Heaven is a wonderful and peaceful place, no matter where you are, but the river is one of my favorite places to be. I love to watch the water move by and to listen to the amazing sounds that it makes. I look at my reflection in the water and just get lost in my thoughts. Momaw told me that my mommy has always done the same thing! Momaw told me that my mommy grew up really close to a river and that my mommy loved the water. When my mommy was sad or lonely, she would always go to the water, and it would make her feel better. It was fun to talk about that and learn how much I really am like my mommy!

Momaw told me all kinds of things about my mommy. Momaw told me what my mommy was like growing up; she explained to me what Mommy looked like and told me all about her favorite things. Even though I never got to meet my mommy, I feel like I know her because of the things that both Jesus and Momaw have told me about her.

It was fun meeting a bunch of other people too. There were people that Momaw knew that I didn't know—family members who had died before my mommy was even born. So Momaw and I would talk to those people, and she would often tell them what my mommy was like. Momaw would use my similarities to my mommy as an example for them. There was a big group of people that we got to talk to in this way. They were grandparents, aunts, uncles, and all kinds of old friends and family members. One of them was Momaw's husband; he died when my mommy's daddy was only twelve years old! It was a fantastic family reunion; I'm so glad that I got to be a part of that.

I will miss my mommy until she gets to live here with me and my new family and friends, but I really love this place. I did not live on earth very long, but I still can't imagine anything on earth being any better than living here! There certainly can't be anything more beautiful and peaceful than this marvelous place that Jesus has made for me to live in. It is going to be so much fun when Jesus brings Mommy here. I can't wait to take her around and introduce her to all of her family that is waiting on her here. But for right now, she is still living her life on earth. Jesus says there are other ways that she can get to know me, and He tells me that she thinks about me all of the time.

Chapter Three

Problems Outside of Paradise

One day, I was sitting in my favorite spot by the river. I was getting ready to find Momaw and talk more about Mommy when I noticed Jesus walking toward me. He said that He needed to talk to me about my mommy. He said that she had been having an especially hard time and was really missing me. Jesus said that she was extra sad and that she was thinking about me all of the time. He said that she was crying a lot and that she was having a hard time focusing on the rest of her life.

I was sad to hear that news for two reasons. The first reason, of course, was because I love my mommy so much. I didn't want my mommy to be sad about me. I wanted her to know that I was in heaven and that I was very happy. But that news made me sad for my brothers and sisters also. They were—and still are—in the world below with her, and they needed her to be happy so that she could enjoy them while they grew up. I wanted her to think of me and remember me, but I didn't want her thoughts of me to make her sad. Jesus patted me on the back and comforted me.

I still think about how sad my mommy is. I know that my mommy has a life that is more than just thinking about me. I am still very concerned about her spending her days thinking of me and being sad instead of raising my brothers and sisters (Mommy had more babies after me). My siblings are not in heaven with Jesus like I am; they need Mommy to help guide them through life. If she is sad all of the time, she cannot help them with all of the things that they need her for. Yes, Mommy being too sad is still a real problem.

On that day when I was by the river, Jesus explained to me that my mommy still felt like it was all her fault that I was not there with her anymore. He said that was why she was so sad. I'm not sure that I understood why she felt that way, but I knew that I didn't want her to worry about me. It really didn't matter to me why I was in heaven or why I left the earth. I knew how I got heaven. I knew I was safe in the arms of Jesus! It was so amazing how He carried me all the way here; I was so safe and warm. I felt nothing but peace and happiness.

Now, I am so happy here, and things for me are so perfect that nothing on earth can compare with what I have here. There's really no need for my mommy to feel sad that I'm here. I wish that I could tell her that somehow! But now that I live in heaven, I can't just go see my mommy any point that I want to. In fact, since I came to heaven before I was even born, I've never been able to see my mommy. All that I have is the memory of seeing her face before Jesus carried me here to my new home. I can't talk to my mommy, but I desperately want to tell her that I am all right and that she needs to live her life.

When I spoke with Jesus that day by the river, I told Jesus that if there was anything that I could do to make my mommy happy, I would be so happy to do it! Then Jesus told me that there was something that I could do. He said that He had an idea, and He wanted to know if I was willing to do something to help my mommy out. My answer was very quick and very enthusiastic. I said, "Yes!" That day, I couldn't wait to hear what Jesus had to say!

♦ ♦ ♦

Jesus started by reminding me that there was no way for me to go to live with my mommy. She lived in the world below, and I lived in heaven. There was no changing that until my mommy's life on earth was done, and she came to live here with me in heaven. But Jesus said that there was a way that I could visit my mommy for just a little while. He said this wasn't something that He offers very often. But Jesus said that sometimes some divine intervention was needed when people missed other people who were in heaven so badly that they had problems living their lives.

Jesus explained to me that I was going to visit Mommy in one of her dreams. She would not know that it was real. For her, it would just be a dream. Jesus said that because she was a human on earth, Mommy would not be able to understand that the dream could be real. But Jesus said that the dream was a way that I could spend some time with my mommy and help her to understand that I was fine, that I didn't blame her for anything, and that she would get to meet me one day in heaven. I thought that this was a perfect plan, and I could not wait to meet my mommy!

The plan was exciting, but when I thought about it, I also got nervous. I was finally going to see my mommy! Even though this wasn't really like "meeting" her, and she wouldn't even realize that her dream was real, it was still real for me. Then many questions rushed through my mind. What was the first thing that I would do? Would she recognize me? What would I say? What would she say? Would she be upset? Would she be happy to see me?

Jesus and Momaw both told me that I needed to stop thinking about meeting Mommy. Momaw sat and talked to me. Momaw reminded me what my mommy was like. She told me that when I met Mommy, I should just do and say whatever came naturally. Everything would be all right. It did not matter what I said or did or what she said or did; the only thing that mattered was that we were going to spend time together. What mattered was that Mommy would wake up from the dream with a new understanding of who and—more importantly—where I was and how good life could still be for her too. I became excited again. Meeting my mommy was going to be so much fun!

Chapter Four

What a Dream!

The time had come. I was finally going to get to spend some time with my mommy. Even though it wasn't quite the normal way, and it wasn't going to be for very long, I was so excited! Mommy was already asleep on earth, and Jesus said that it was time for me to join her in a dream. Mommy had no idea she was about to meet the child that she never knew.

Suddenly, I found myself in a world that I had never been in before. It was almost as pretty as heaven but not completely. There were a lot of similarities, but it was still not quite the same. Of all the places on earth that my mommy could be in her dream, she was on a beach. I guess Momaw was right. Mommy really did love the water as much as I did.

I found myself walking along the shore of a beautiful body of water. As I took each step, my feet sunk down lightly in the sand, while the waves crashed into the sand near my feet. The sound that the water made was amazing. There was a smell in the air that made the dream so peaceful, happy, and relaxing. I looked way out into the distance and saw some dolphins jumping out of the water; they looked like they were having fun. Although not as breathtaking as my home, this world was definitely magnificent.

As I was taking in the beauty of this place, I heard something—another sound that my ears had never heard before. It was not a joyous sound, nor was it a peaceful sound. The sound was an intense, desperate sobbing. The weeping was so powerful that it seemed to shake the entire ground. I looked to where the sound was coming from, and I saw a very beautiful woman. I knew her immediately. The woman was my mommy! I ran to her so quickly that it seemed like I was floating. When she looked up at me, it seemed that she knew me also. Her eyes were fixed so intently on the sight of me running to her, but she looked very confused. Deep within her, she knew who I was, but she also realized that I was not actually there. She knew she was dreaming. Mommy was so overwhelmed by the sight of her child that she simply stood and stared at me.

I was almost to my mommy. I was so close, and I just could not wait one more minute to grab her and give her the biggest hug that anyone has ever given to another person. But I noticed that she was turning away. Suddenly, for some reason, she stopped looking at me. It seemed like my mommy wasn't as happy to see me as I was to see her, but why not? When I got close enough to touch her, I noticed that Mommy had not only turned her eyes but had also turned her entire body. She was also hunched over. It was like she couldn't bear the thought of me being there.

I did not understand why Mommy couldn't look at me. Did she not like the way that I looked? Did she not believe that she was really seeing me? The hunger for the answers to these questions was just as strong as the need to see her. I began to speak and said, "Ummm…h-h-hi." Mommy still did not turn to face me.

"Who are you?" she asked, knowing that she knew the answer.

"I'm Joshua!" I answered her. "I'm your child! I didn't live long enough to be born, but you're my mommy. I saw you right before Jesus carried me to heaven." With those words, my mommy turned even farther away from me and hunched over even more. Her body became even tenser. Not only did her eyes and body turn from me, but she also seemed to melt into the sand that was beneath our feet. Her sobbing became uncontrollable, and she was shaking terribly. I was beginning to wonder if my presence was going to help Mommy at all.

It seemed like my words were only making Mommy upset, so I knew that there was only one thing left that I could do. I walked over to her and put my hand on her shoulder. I could feel the grief that seemed to be exploding from within her. She was still sobbing when I decided that just my hand on her shoulder was not enough. I wrapped my arms around Mommy's neck and hugged her. Oh, how I had been waiting for this moment! Mommy didn't pull away from me, but she still wouldn't look at me. She just cried and cried for what seemed like forever. I had no reason to cry, nor did I feel any need to be healed. But this hug seemed to be healing and helping my mommy. When the hug was over, she finally looked at me. We both just stared at each other for what seemed like eternity (but it was actually about five or ten minutes).

"Why? How? Surely this can't be real!" Mommy jumped up and spoke so quickly, but she did not give me any time to answer. "I know it is you, but you can't be here. You died! You were never born. How are you here? I must be dead too. That's it. Have I died? What happened to me? How did I—"

"Mommy, please stop for a minute! Just listen to me for a minute, and I can explain," I said. I tried to calm her down. I grabbed her hand and motioned for her to have a seat in the sand again. Then we settled into the sand and watched the waves hit the shore. I explained to her where I had come from. I told her that Jesus, Momaw, and I were worried about her because she had been so sad. "I just love you so much, so I told Jesus that I would come visit you so that you would know that I am all right and that there's no reason to be sad!" I said.

Mommy began to cry again, but this time, her tears weren't uncontrollable. "When I first saw you," she began to explain, "I knew who you were, but I was just so ashamed."

"So that's why you couldn't look at me!" I exclaimed.

"You died because I did not protect you. From the very moment you died, I knew it was wrong, but I didn't know what else to do. I just wanted you back. I wanted to hold you, love you, raise you, and watch you grow, but there was no way for those things to happen. You were gone, and I was left with nothing but guilt, shame, and remorse. I wanted so badly to just tell you how much I loved you, but I knew that I no longer had any right to do so."

I told my mommy that she had no reason to feel this way. She desperately needed to know that I held no grudges against her and that I was happy. I knew she loved me, and in my mind, there was no reason for any negativity between the two of us. I knew that Jesus was right and that Mommy desperately needed me to visit her. I said a quick prayer and thanked Jesus for sending me to talk to Mommy.

I began to fill her in on the truth. I told her this: "Mommy, I have a life, and it is not here on this earth. I am very happy! I spend all of my time by a beautiful river, talking to Jesus or some person from our family. One of my best friends is Momaw! You know her; she was your grandma! We talk about you all of the time, and she tells me how much she loves you and all about your childhood. Jesus explained to me that I needed to be with Him instead of with you and that you would join us one day." I watched her face as I talked; it changed from shameful to curious. Finally, I saw some relief in her eyes. Her body finally relaxed, and love replaced the guilt in her eyes.

I had to get this very important message to Mommy before my time was up. As I grabbed her hand and looked deep into her eyes, I said, "Mommy, I really need you to know something. Jesus told me that you are very sad and that you live a lot of your life in tears and depression. You have to stop that! There is no reason for you to feel guilty. I want you to be happy and to live your life. My brothers and sisters need you.

That is why Jesus sent me here today. We both need you to stop being so sad. Mommy, please remember me, be happy, and know that my life is very good."

Then she cried and cried and cried. But the crying was softer than before. I think that her tears were sad tears mixed with happy tears. I think she was beginning to heal. I saw peace all over her face, and her whole body began to change. Mommy looked up and stared into my eyes. I saw a smile grow on her face, and I saw a light in her eyes that had not been there before. I think it may have been in her eyes a long time ago but had been covered by the darkness of her sadness. It was the most wonderful thing to see the light return! She hugged me so tightly that it seemed like she would never let go. I didn't want her to.

Mommy and I decided to walk down closer to the water. We walked just close enough to get our feet wet in the waves. We walked hand in hand and just talked. She told me all about my siblings and my new daddy. She told me about the memorial service that they had had for me and about how much I was talked about and loved. Mommy told me that I looked a lot like my big brother and that we had a lot of similarities. I said I couldn't wait to meet him and all of my other siblings. She said there was even a little tribute to me in her new house so that every time any person in my family looked at it, he or she could think of me. I knew that I loved my family even though I had never met them, and I felt very close to them. They all seemed so fun.

The Journey

As we watched the sun go down at the far end of the water, we knew that our time together was coming to an end. Knowing that the end was near brought us sadness, but it was not the same kind of sadness that we had experienced before. Neither of us wanted this to be over; we both were enjoying our time so much. However, we knew that we did not belong in this world together. I would go back to heaven, and she was needed back in her life. My daddy and my siblings needed her. My grandma needed her. She had a lot of people in her life that depended so heavily upon her. I looked at Mommy and hugged her. I told her that I loved her so very much and that I would be waiting for her in heaven. I asked her to tell my siblings and my daddy that I loved them very much. I wanted her to tell my grandma that I loved her too. She cried and told me that she loved me very much and that she was so glad that we had gotten this time together. Mommy and I hugged each other tightly. We hugged like there was nothing else to do. We hugged until our time was up. Then we were separated once more. I found myself sitting back by the gorgeous river in heaven. Jesus and Momaw were sitting there. They were watching me stare at the water. I ran to them and hugged them; I was so thankful to Jesus for letting me have such a great time with my mommy! Then I wondered what my mommy was doing at that moment.

Chapter Five

A New Friend

Jesus, Momaw, and I sat down by the river to talk. As the three of us gazed at the beauty of the water, I saw the smiles on their faces as they looked at me. I did not have to tell them what happened in my visit with Mommy because Jesus already knew what had happened. He knew before I even left! (Jesus knows everything that will happen for all of time!) But as I looked at their big smiles, which were as beautiful as the sparkling water that we sat beside, I had to share my story with them.

"It was so wonderful!" I said as I began telling them. "Mommy is so pretty! She is so nice and fun! It is so pretty there too. It is not as gorgeous as heaven but still beautiful!" I spoke so quickly that they could have thought I was going crazy. But they know better. I was just so excited; I had never felt this kind of excitement before. I had just met my mom for the first time!

"Slow down, dear one," Momaw said. "We're in heaven. Time will not run out. I'm so glad you had a good time with your mom. She really is a wonderful person."

"Yes, she really is—better than I even dreamed she would be. We had such a good time walking in the sand and getting to know each other. She seemed so sad when I first saw her, but I think she is better now—at least a little bit. Do you think that she will be all right now that she has met me, Jesus?"

"Yes, my child," He began speaking. His voice was so calming and reassuring; everything about Him was just so amazing. "Meeting you helped your mother understand that you really are here with Me and that you are safe and happy. She has a very long road ahead of her, but she can see more clearly now, and that is all thanks to you, precious one," Jesus said. Jesus was so amazing to talk to.

As reassuring as talking to Jesus was, there was something that He said that made me a little bit worried. Why did my mommy have a long road ahead of her? What exactly did that mean? Were things still bad for her? Should I go back and see her again? Would Jesus even let me go back again? My joy suddenly turned into many more questions—some of which made me very confused to even think about.

As I began to form my questions into words, Jesus told me that He had to go. He had a very important journey that He needed to take. He said that it would be one that I would appreciate and that He would explain things more when He got back. Momaw and I waved good-bye to Jesus and looked at each other to decide what we would do while we waited for Him to return. We decided that it would be fun for the both of us if she told me more about when my mommy was a little girl. Oh, how I loved these talks that we had!

♦ ♦ ♦

When Jesus came back later that day, He was not alone. He had a new friend with Him—one that I have never seen before. What was even more exciting than having a new friend in heaven was that Jesus brought her straight to me so that I could meet her first!

"Joshua, I would like to introduce you to Sierra," He proudly declared when they got close to me. I wondered what my connection to Sierra was. Was she my sister? No, that didn't seem right. Maybe she was my cousin. Perhaps our mommies were friends, so Jesus just wanted us to meet. I was very glad to have a new friend, but I didn't understand why I was getting the pleasure of meeting this new friend before anyone else in heaven.

I noticed Sierra looking around in amazement as she noticed all of the beauty in heaven. I could tell that she must have been pretty young when she left her life on earth. Sometimes, it was hard to tell ages in heaven because there is no age in heaven. (It doesn't matter how old a person was when he or she died. Everyone comes to heaven just as people. Age isn't a thing that really matters to anyone here.) However, sometimes I could tell, and Sierra definitely had not lived on earth for very long. There was something about her that was familiar. I wondered what it was that was familiar.

Sierra interrupted my thoughts by running up and saying hello. "Hi! I'm so excited to meet you! Jesus told me all about you while He was bringing me here. He said that you and I were going to be great friends!" She spoke to me but looked around in amazement. It seemed that she was taking everything in and that she was falling completely in love with her wonderful and new home. I finally figured out who she reminded me of. She reminded me of myself when I first came here!

As I realized how much my new friend reminded me of myself, I caught a glimpse of Jesus and Momaw. They were talking to each other but looking at me and smiling proudly. I wondered what they were talking about. There was certainly something going on that was different, yet everything felt so familiar. I couldn't figure out what exactly was going on, but I was sure that it would all be revealed soon; everything always got figured out in heaven. Things always worked together just perfectly. I said that to Jesus once, and He told me that He had said something like that in His word that He left for His people who were still living to read. He explained that it was a big book. The big book was full of some of the wonderful things that He had done so that people could grow closer to Him until they came to heaven to live. I thought that He was so devoted to His people; I always loved to hear how He always made sure that everyone had a way to Him!

"Sierra, this is Joshua," Jesus said to her. "The two of you have a lot in common. You both lived very short lives, but many great things will happen because of your existence."

So now I knew what was familiar about my new friend. She reminded me of myself because she came to heaven in the same way that I did. I wondered if Jesus let her look at her mommy for a minute before bringing her here, like He did for me.

"Hi, Sierra. It's so nice to meet you. You are going to love living here! We have so much fun, and everything is just perfect."

Jesus told us to sit down so that we could talk. Momaw also joined us. She was beaming with excitement because Jesus had already told her what was going to happen between Sierra, me, and our mommies. She looked like she was going to burst from excitement! Sierra and I sat down, and I patted for Momaw to come sit close to me.

Jesus explained that Sierra and I both had died because of something called "abortion." That is when a mommy doesn't want to be pregnant with her baby, so she has a doctor take the baby out of her belly. The only problem with that is that the baby can't live without staying in the mommy's belly, so the baby goes to heaven to live with Jesus. But eventually the mommy starts to miss her baby and wishes that she could hold her son or daughter. The problem is that it is too late; the baby is gone. That's why my mommy was so sad when I met her.

However, with Jesus, that bad news never stayed bad. There was always a good ending when it came to those He has made His children. Sierra and I didn't have long lives with our mommies, but now we get to live for eternity in heaven, and heaven is so much better! Now, our lives matter here in heaven, and they matter to our mommies too.

"The two of you are going to become great friends, but that is not the end of the story," Jesus told us. "There is even more exciting news! Your mothers are going to become great friends too. Joshua, your mother has already started to heal from feeling guilty over your death, and she is going to help Sierra's mother do the same. After that, the two of them are going to start helping many other people learn that all of their babies are safe and happy here in heaven with us. They are going to work together to show many people how much I love them and forgive them. These people will all come to know Me because of what your mothers will do. Do you see how important your lives were, even though they were so short?"

After hearing Jesus speak, I began to understand something that I had not thought about before. I loved my life in heaven, and I knew that I was important because I was loved by God, but Jesus helped me to understand that I had a life among the living too and that I was important among the living. I didn't live very long—a short seventeen weeks, to be exact—but God gave me worth, and even though I went to heaven, He used and was going to use my life for His good. I had never thought about my life among the living because I wasn't ever able to do anything there, but I realized that I was important there too!

Now I know that I still am important there, and God is so amazing that He is letting people think about me. He is still using my short life today. God is so good; I am so happy!

Chapter Six

A Praise Session

As I thought about how great God is and how happy I was in my home and my life, I decided to start listening to the angels singing praises to God.

This was such a fun thing to do, and I still do it now. The angels are always singing in heaven because God is just so amazing. Heaven is an incredible place to be, but the most important thing about heaven is praising God, because He made everyone and provides this awesome life that we have. It really is impossible to tell someone about heaven without communicating that God is the center of heaven.

The angels are gorgeous creatures! They shine so brightly as they sing praises to God and as His glory reflects off of them. There are no words to describe how beautiful they are. The voices of the angels are just as beautiful as the sight of the angels themselves. They do not sing as a human would. Instead, their voices seem to be even more powerful as they worship their Creator. Sometimes, it seems like they aren't even singing any words. It is just magnificent praise, and it makes God so very happy. Listening to the angels makes me get lost in my thoughts. First, I think of how beautiful they sound. Then my thoughts quickly go to how amazing God is. He loves us all more than anything, and He gives us everything that we need and even so much more!

I stood there listening to the angels, and I began thinking of my mommy and her new friend, Sierra's mommy. God was going to help them both and then use them to help other people, even though they had done some terrible things in their lives. I realized that there just wasn't any person or thing among the living or in heaven that was better or more amazing than God!

I was so lost in my thoughts and my worship that I did not realize that some of my other friends were standing around me worshipping too. (You see, people in heaven are all friends—well, more like family! It doesn't matter what time period someone lived in or how old someone was when he or she came to heaven; if you arrive in heaven, you're family. We all have a very close relationship with each other.)

Standing right beside me was my friend Joseph. Joseph and I liked to talk about our families among the living. He had a big family; he had eleven brothers and a bunch of sisters too! His daddy loved him more than any of his other brothers, and Joseph had many problems because of that. His brothers got really jealous and did some really bad things to him. They even sent him away to be a slave in another town! My friend didn't see his family for many years after that, but when he was reunited with his family, he told them that he was all right and that everything that had happened was all a part of God's plan to keep them safe and happy.

Then I looked to my left and saw my very good friend David. I liked being around him! When David told me about his time among the living, it seemed like he did everything! He was a very poor shepherd when he was very young; then he lived with a king, and then he was a soldier. He was a king too. He did many things, including writing his own praise songs to God. A lot of the things that he wrote even ended up in that book that God had left as His word for the people who were still living. David and I had and still have a special bond, because when he was living, he had a child who died very young. So he knew what my mommy was feeling. David told me that when my mommy got to heaven, he was going to tell her that he helped watch over me in honor of his own son who had died so young. David's son is a really neat person too. On that day, he was standing by his daddy, holding his hand. Now David's son and I play together often. The river is our favorite place to play!

Soon, I felt a hand on each of my shoulders. I turned to see some more "adoptive parents" of mine; their names were Mary and Joseph. When they were alive, these wonderful people were the parents of Jesus. How special is that? Their lives were not easy, but they trusted God, and when they got to heaven, He blessed them for the hard times that they had endured. There were many times that I had spent hours talking to them about the childhood of Jesus. I sure loved listening to them talk about their lives!

Standing beside Mary and Joseph was their good friend Lazarus. When Lazarus was alive, he had been a very close friend to Jesus during His time as a minister. Lazarus has a special story also. Lazarus died when Jesus was going from town to town, teaching the people about who He was and how they needed Him. To show the people how powerful Jesus really was, Jesus brought Lazarus back to life. Lazarus had been dead for three whole days! That was always a fun story to hear, because Lazarus talked about how he told his sisters that he didn't want to be back among the living because it was so amazing in heaven. I think it helped his sisters—who had now joined him and were standing in our group—to understand how special heaven is and how it's better to come to heaven than it is to keep on living.

Another person who understood how living in heaven is so much better than living on earth was Stephen. In his time on earth, Stephen had a really bad time right before he died. Stephen was a preacher, and he went around and told people how good God was and how they needed to live their lives for Him. (It is hard for me to imagine not needing God, but there are people among the living who do not think that they need God.) These people got very mad about the things that Stephen said. They became so angry that they killed him! However, as Stephen was dying, he looked up into the sky and saw Jesus standing up and waiting to usher him into heaven.

Steph Loughman

One of Stephen's best friends in heaven is a man named Paul. It is really neat to hear the story of how they became such good friends because Paul was one of the men who was involved in Stephen's death. You see, while the men were killing Stephen, Paul watched over all of their coats for them. At that time, his name was Saul, and he didn't understand who God was. But one day, Jesus spoke to Saul, changed his name to Paul, and changed his life completely. Paul lived the rest of his life telling people about God and how much they needed Him. One of my favorite stories to listen to is about how Stephen ran to Paul upon his arrival to heaven and how the two of them became such close friends.

I looked around and realized that many others had joined us. The crowd grew larger and larger. I loved all of these people so much, and I loved to hear their stories. Each and every person in our group was special and had an amazing tale of arriving in heaven. However, all of the stories, no matter how different they might be, were centered on one thing: God was always to be praised. He was the God who provided grace and the mercy; He paved the way for all of these people and their stories to be redeemed. In heaven, we all know that God is to be praised always.

So that is what we all did that day. As the crowd grew larger and larger, we all stood gazing upon the awesomeness of God. We listened as the angels sang His glory, and we joined in with the angels to make one voice. Some people were kneeling, while others had raised their hands. Some people lay flat on the ground. Some of us who stood had our arms around each other, swaying back and forth. Regardless of how we held our bodies, we all did the same thing. We all praised our amazing God. We shouted His glory and worshipped His goodness. It was not our voices that sang. Our hearts sang. It was a beautiful scene that made me fall in love with God even more. Just when I think that it is not possible to love Jesus more, things happen, and I fall deeper in love with Him. He truly is more amazing than I can ever find words to describe.

Chapter Seven

Family Ties

I was still singing in my heart and worshipping God when Momaw approached me and said, "Jesus said that there are two more people on their way here and that He wants us to meet them."

Awesome! I was always excited to meet new people when they came to heaven; in fact, I often sat near the gates and watched as new souls entered into eternity. However, I wondered why it was important that Momaw and I meet these new people immediately upon their arrival. I thought that there must be some exciting reason that it was important for me to get to meet them before anyone else.

Then I saw Jesus walking toward us with the two new souls. They looked young, like Sierra and I were at first, but somehow different. I didn't think that they came to heaven the same way that Sierra and I had, but I certainly saw some similarities. I ran to meet Jesus and my new friends. "Hi! I'm Joshua; it's so nice to meet you!" I yelled as I ran toward them.

When Momaw caught up with me, Jesus introduced our new friends to us. "This is Brett and Lissa," Jesus said. He

The Journey

then turned to them and said words that almost knocked me down: "Dear ones, Joshua is your brother."

Brother? Sister? Here in heaven? I wasn't sure how I felt about this. I was happy to have siblings here with me, but what would their being here do to Mommy? She was already so sad that I was here. How was she going to deal with having three children in heaven? Oh, poor Mommy!

"H-h-h-how, Jesus? Did Mommy send them here the same way that she sent me here?" I asked. Jesus assured me that my siblings had not come to heaven in the same way that I had. He told me that my mommy had a few miscarriages, which means that the babies died before they were born. He explained that Mommy was going to be very sad that they were here, but after meeting me in the dream, she understood that all three of us were with Jesus and that we were all right. She would mourn for them, but she would be all right. Although I was so sad to know that Mommy would have to go through mourning again, I was very relieved that she was going to recover. I was excited again! My focus turned to my new siblings. I got to know them and showed them around our wonderful home.

I got to introduce Brett and Lissa to Momaw. She hugged them and welcomed them to heaven. She was just as happy to meet them as she was to meet me. Momaw was so kind to Brett and Lissa. It was great having such a fun grandma in heaven when Brett and Lissa came. She and I spent a little bit of time telling my new siblings about Mommy so that they could get to know Mommy as they waited to meet her.

My siblings looked around at their new home in amazement—just like all new souls do. Lissa clung to Brett very closely but looked around with very wide eyes. Brett was obviously the stronger of the two and proudly held on to our sister; I could tell that they were very close, even though their lives had been painfully short. Brett asked, "Can Joshua take us over to that beautiful river, Jesus?" I knew he was definitely my brother and that we were going to have so much fun.

Momaw stayed with Jesus; Lissa, Brett, and I walked to the river. I talked about how awesome it is to live in heaven and how beautiful heaven is. Lissa didn't really talk too much, but I could tell that she was just taking it all in. She would look at me, then look at Brett, and then stare all around her. Poor thing—she just wasn't used to being in heaven yet, but I knew that she would come around and that she would be all right. Until she felt comfortable, Brett would be her support. That's what big brothers are for.

As we sat down by my beautiful river, I could tell that Brett and Lissa loved it as much as I did. I was so happy to have siblings to share the river with. I told them about Jesus letting me visit our mommy in a dream. They listened in amazement as I retold that amazing day at the beach. I kept looking at Lissa as I spoke. She was struggling to listen to all of this. There is no real sadness here in heaven, nor are there tears. But Lissa looked like she might be feeling sad. I could tell that she was grappling to find the right words, but she finally mouthed a simple "Why?" Her little eyes were just so confused and unsure.

"Why are we here instead of with her, Joshua? I want to know Mommy! I want to snuggle up in her lap and feel her hug me. I want to hear her tell me that she loves me. I mean, don't get me wrong—this place is absolutely unbelievable, but why couldn't we have some time with Mommy? Did we do something wrong?" Lissa asked me.

She asked such hard questions, and she really needed to hear the answers. I badly wanted to help her, but I wasn't sure that I was able to. After all, that was my first day of being a big brother. As always, I didn't need to worry. Before I could speak, I heard Jesus come up behind me. He was very ready to help Lissa understand.

"Dear one, climb up on my lap, and let me tell you a story" He said to her. He sat down, and Lissa let go of Brett and quickly climbed onto Jesus's lap and into His loving arms. Brett and I gathered around to sit at His feet, and He began to talk.

Jesus explained to us that the world below was filled with something awful called "sin." It was a terrible thing that God could not stand. He said that because of sin, people had to die. However, things didn't end there; there was good news! God sent His Son, Jesus, to take the punishment for everyone's sins so that there would be a way for them to come to heaven when they died. Jesus had taken care of everything for us all!

"But, Jesus," Lissa interrupted, "that explains why people die and how people come here to heaven. But that's not what I wanted to know. I want to know why I can't be with my mommy. Am I being punished or something?"

Jesus hugged her tightly and said, "No, dear one, you are not being punished—quite the opposite, in fact. You see, you were ready to be here. Your life down below—as short as it was—is going to be used greatly in helping your mother learn about Me; then she's going to use what she learned from her experience to help other people come to know Me so that they can come to heaven too. You see, dear one, because of you, a lot of people are going to be able to come live here with us. So it is not that you are being punished or even that your mother is being punished. You are just so important that you need to be here! You are so very special, my little one."

Lissa said that those words from Jesus felt like a big hug. That conversation with Jesus was just what she needed to hear, and she understood why she was in heaven and separated from Mommy. She realized she could stop worrying, have fun, and enjoy life. I decided that it was a good time to take her and Brett around and show them heaven; I was also excited to introduce them to all of my friends and show my friends that I had a brother and a sister!

We had so much fun running from place to place. I introduced my siblings to the angels, and we sat and listened to the angels' singing for a long time. Their voices were just so pretty! I introduced Brett and Lissa to some of my favorite angel friends. I think that my siblings really liked their new angel friends.

After listening to the angels for a little while, we went to visit some of my other friends—the ones whose lives were used and talked about in God's book to all people. My friend David was very excited to meet Brett and Lissa. He struggled a lot when he was alive, and he understood how someone living in heaven could help lead others to Jesus. My brother, sister, and David talked for a long time about life on earth and about how much better life in heaven was. They talked about people, angels, and—most importantly—how precious Jesus was to them. I thought David would probably be my siblings' best friend.

Brett, Lissa, and I spent that entire day running all around heaven and meeting different people and angels. Sierra joined us for a lot of the time too. My brother and sister had so much fun learning about their new home and getting to know everyone. As they stood in awe of heaven, I watched them, and I was in awe of them. I was so happy to have them in heaven. I couldn't wait to spend every day getting to know them better.

Suddenly, I noticed where we were standing. My siblings and I were back at the very place that we met—the magnificent gates where all souls enter heaven. I often sat there, waiting to meet new friends and see who was coming to this amazing place. I decided that I should let my siblings in on my secret. I loved to watch new souls enter heaven, but that wasn't the only reason I sat there.

Although I loved being in heaven, and I totally trusted that Jesus had everything under control, there were times when I just missed Mommy. It was on those days that I sat by the gates and watched. It was and still is wonderful to see all the new souls enter heaven, but I am also watching for Mommy. (I still look forward to the day when she will arrive in heaven. I love her so much and am so excited to hug her and tell her that I love her. I remember when Jesus said that Mommy was afraid I wouldn't want to see her. Nothing could be further from the truth. I can't wait to see her again!) So there I would sit, watching the gate. Now I had company who was just as anxious as I was to see Mommy. I knew that we would talk, laugh, make new friends, and have an amazing life in heaven together. But I also knew that my siblings and I would sit and wait for Mommy's arrival. One day, we would finally be reunited with our mommy.

Lissa screamed excitedly, "Joshua, the gates are opening! Could it be Mommy? Do you think today could be the day?"

Brett, Lissa, and I stood, holding hands and watching as the glorious gates opened. We hoped that day would be the day.

I still often think to myself, "Maybe today will be the day. Only time will tell."

Mommy's Journey

Even after death, a mother and her child are forever connected. There is a deep bond that cannot be destroyed even when the two are living in two separate worlds. Joshua loved his mommy and would do anything to protect her, even though he had never really met her.

While Joshua's journey took him to heaven and allowed him to meet Jesus and a great deal of new friends, his mother had a different journey. Joshua's mother's journey was one of much pain and regret. However, once she was able to deal with the pain of her past, she was able to see that her son was safe and happy and that she was just as connected to him as she was to her living children. In comparing these separate journeys, it becomes very evident how similar they really are.

Chapter One

My Changing World

Who knew that two little lines on a stick that you take into the bathroom could change your life forever? Two lines and one word have more power than some can even imagine at times. Pregnant, I wondered how on earth I was going to handle a new baby and all of the work and emotions that come with it. How was I going to tell my family that I had yet another baby coming, especially so soon? I just started a new job and have just begun rebuilding my life. I was finally going to get things set straight for my son and myself after years of living a wild lifestyle. How is this pregnancy going to impact everything that I had worked so hard for in the past few months?

Ever since the day I discovered that pregnancy, I have asked myself and thought deeply about those questions for many years. However, the time came for me to make my decision. Should I go ahead and tell my family that I was going to have a baby and begin making the necessary changes to my life to prepare for this new life, or do I take the easy way out and have an abortion? That question weighed heavily on my mind but only for about five minutes.

Steph Loughman

I have always been a person that supported a woman's right to end her pregnancy, but I didn't think that I would ever have an abortion. I have made a lot of mistakes in my life, but when I do something wrong, I own up to it and do whatever I need to remedy the wrong. So for me, there was no choice. I was pregnant, so I was going to have a baby. I decided that I will take whatever consequences came with telling everyone, and I will love my baby and raise him or her to be a wonderful person.

For four months, I carried my child in my womb. I took care of myself so that my baby would be healthy. I held my stomach as it expanded with my growing child, and I talked to the baby many times. I became very well aware that this was my child, and I grew to love him or her very much. However, I soon found out that all it took to shatter my life was one moment of weakness.

My situation was not a good one. My baby's father was not a good man. He was happy about the pregnancy because it kept me tied to him forever. He liked that because he enjoyed having someone to push around. He was a very dangerous man. When I finally pushed him out of my life, he still came around because I was carrying his child. He would stalk me and seemed to be always watching me. One night, I had a friend over to keep me company and to keep me from being so scared, and she saw him peeking through the windows. It was not a healthy lifestyle, and I knew that there was only one way to get rid of this man for good. I had to have an abortion. Of course, he would kill me if he knew, so I decided I would tell him that I had had a miscarriage. Then maybe I would finally be done with this man forever.

To add to my self-description from before, I have always been the type of person to make a choice and stick with it. I knew what I was going to do was wrong, but I also knew that this was what had to be done to protect my son and myself. I also knew that this new baby would not have a good life because his or her father would be sure to make both me and my baby miserable because of his own selfish, arrogant ways. This is what I told myself so that I could push past the consequences and do what I needed to do without giving it another thought. I was sure that abortion was my only freedom from this man, so I made the phone calls and began the process.

The whole thing seemed to go so smoothly in the planning stages. Living in a smaller city, I had to drive to the next county for the procedure, but the procedure really didn't seem to be a big deal. It seemed as if the procedure was going to go fast and easy, just like all the protestors for women's rights promised. The procedure was even covered by my health insurance; I wasn't even going to have to pay one single penny for the procedure. What could possibly go wrong…right? All of the health-care professionals kept everything secret for me, and it was just all too easy. But I knew little about the horror that this one event would bring to my life.

I thought that I would have this procedure and then go about the rest of my life. It never occurred to me that there might be aftereffects. I fully comprehended what the procedure was going to do, but somehow I allowed myself to push

Steph Loughman

the reality of what was going on deep into my mind. I told myself that it would be fine and that the procedure was not only the best thing possible for my son and myself but that it was the only option that I had as well. Time was up for everything that I knew—for the way I had been living, for the man who was controlling me, and for everything that I knew. The moment the procedure began was the last minute for everything that I knew. My whole world changed in that minute—in that one event.

Chapter Two

The Procedure

I was pretty far along in my pregnancy—seventeen weeks to be exact—so it was not going to be a short procedure by any means. First, I had to see the doctor in his office. The very first thing that he did was an ultrasound. I thought to myself, "This is just great!" I had done everything possible to make myself believe that this baby was anything but a human, and then I had to see an ultrasound.

As I got lost in my thoughts, I noticed the doctor, his nurse, and my mom looking at me as if they were waiting for my reply on something. Mom put her hand on my shoulder and repeated the doctor's words: "Would you like to see the ultrasound, honey?" I knew I had to pull myself together and focus on what needed to be done. I told myself I could do it.

"No! I just can't!" I said in agitation. So the nurse turned the screen and made it impossible for me to see my unborn child. Everything in me was silently moaning. I wanted nothing more than to look at that screen, see my baby, and run screaming from that room. It was bad enough that the baby had started moving that morning. I had felt small flitters of movement before, but he or she was rolling around and moving like crazy that day. If I had not known better, I would have thought that he or she somehow knew what was going to happen and was begging me not to do it.

I allowed my mind to wander to whatever could to get me past the ultrasound. I was so relieved when it was over. But the ultrasound was only the first event in a long list of events that would prove to be nearly impossible to endure. The nurse asked me to move to another room. My mom and I waited in this small, cold room for what seemed like forever. Finally, the doctor entered the room, and then the true horror began.

In his thick foreign accent, the doctor explained that he would perform a procedure that would essentially begin labor. I would then go home and spend the evening feeling contractions. Then I would return to the hospital in the morning so that he could remove the baby from my womb. Wow! I was able to push things back and force myself to do things that were extremely hard, but surviving this procedure seemed impossible. It all seemed so crazy. I thought that I would go in and have the abortion, and then things would go back to normal. And I'd never have to consider it again. I wondered how I was going to get through that night.

I was in a daze. I don't really remember much about that drive home or about what happened that evening. All that I remember is holding my stomach, telling my child that I was so sorry, and begging him to forgive me. I remember saying that I loved him and that the procedure was the only choice that I had. I think I probably repeated these words all night long.

At some point, I cried myself to sleep, which ushered me into what would be the most horrific day of my life.

The next morning, I awoke early. I had to be at the hospital at an early hour. My mom drove me because I was not going to be able to drive myself home. I was not allowed to eat, but she stopped and got herself some food and coffee on the way. Oh, what I would have done to be able to have a bite or two!

When we arrived at the hospital, I was informed that I was to report to labor and delivery. My heart sank. I had been feeling contractions since leaving the doctor's office yesterday, and then I had to go to the labor and delivery department. When I got to the correct department, I was put in a large room with a bunch of other women. We were all in labor but at different stages. Most had men with them and were excited about having their babies, and then there was me. I was in labor so that my baby could die. I had no choice but to lie there and think about what was going on inside my body. Though I tried desperately to not think about it, I was curious about what my baby was feeling in that moment.

As I lay there thinking about my child—the precious life that was going to end because of my choices—my labor intensified. The contractions were coming closer and closer together, and the pressure was getting harder and harder. At one point, I looked at my mom and told her that I was sure that I was going to have to go into the delivery room and deliver the baby alive. I was terrified of that because I knew that if I were to see my baby and hold him, I would regret the abortion for the rest of my life. I was well aware that if I were to deliver the baby at that point in my pregnancy, he would not survive. I was also well aware that my child was very much alive at that moment because he was rolling around inside my stomach like he was playing a game. Was he telling me good-bye? Maybe he was begging me to stop. There was no stopping at this point—no turning back. This abortion was happening, and it was happening quickly.

At what seemed to be the very last second before I was going to have to push, the nurse came to get me and wheeled me into the operating room. A nurse had already given me some sort of drugs, and I felt very woozy. I saw a bunch of lights in the room, and there were a lot of people busily running around the room. Eventually, a nurse looked at me and said that I would be asleep soon. He wanted me to count backward until I feel asleep. Ten...nine...eight...

I awoke in a smaller room; I was somehow sitting in a chair. My mom waved the nurse over and told her that I was awake. The nurse asked me how I was, and I quickly asked her if it was all over. She sadly shook her head.

It was over—the procedure, the pain, and my child's life. Everything was done. It would be a little while before I realized that a big piece of me had died that day too.

Chapter Three

A New Life

As promised, things went back to normal for me. The constant reminder of the pregnancy was gone, so I was able to push all of the baggage that went along with the procedure to the back of my mind. I thought that I had done pretty well and had put it all behind me. So I went on with life, not allowing myself even the smallest thought of my child. In fact, I never even allowed myself to consider that a life was ever even in my womb.

I had only one more thing left to do to end that chapter of my life. I met with the baby's father to let him know that we no longer had a connection. When he came over, he brought his daughter with him. She was the only reason that I felt bad. My son was so young that he would not ever remember having gone through this, but this young lady was a teenager. She was so excited about getting another younger sibling. I really wished that I did not have to face her with that news.

"I've been trying to get ahold of you. Are you all right? How's my baby doing?" He tried to get close to me. As always, I backed up.

"Uhh...I've been at the hospital." I was going to do this fast, like ripping off a bandage. I could not wait to be done with this part of my life! "I'm sorry to tell you this, but I had a miscarriage. The baby is gone," I told him. I tried unsuccessfully to not look at his daughter. Devastation was written all over her face. She broke my heart.

I'm not sure if he believed me or not. He asked many detailed questions, and I gave whatever answers I could and made up a lot of things to just to go along with my story. I couldn't wait to get out of that conversation! He asked if he could see the baby, tell him good-bye, and hold him; he even wanted to bury the baby. He told me a story about an aunt of his who had had a miscarriage and was able to bury her baby. I had to think quickly, but I still didn't miss a beat and informed him that there were issues and that the doctors had taken the baby quickly. I let him know that I didn't even get to see the baby. I'm still not sure if he had been testing me to see if I was telling the truth or if he was just trying to comprehend the death of his child. Either way, in the end, he bought the story. We said good-bye, and I never heard from him again. That was the only good thing that came out of that whole terrible situation.

I went on with my life as I had planned. I had finally gotten rid of that man and had started over. I went to work every day, and when I came home, I enjoyed spending time with my son. I never gave my abortion or my child another thought. In fact, in some way, I had succeeded in forgetting all about the whole thing. I had moved my life in a new direction and had never looked back. Or so I thought.

It did not take long before tragedy struck again. A short ten days after my abortion, I got a call that I had been expecting for quite some time. My grandma, whom I always called Momaw, had passed away. She had been battling Alzheimer disease for many, many years. She hadn't seen any of us for years; it was a long, heart-wrenching disease. I was very close to Momaw when I was growing up, so I was devastated to hear that she had passed away.

After going back to my hometown for Momaw's funeral, I returned home and tried to resume a normal life. However, I always felt that something was missing. It was as if I was in a constant state of searching, but I could never figure out what I was searching for. I assumed it was because I missed Momaw; I had been so very close to her. But as I always had, I kept plugging away at life and just tried to make things work.

One day, I went to work, and suddenly, I was transferred to a different department. I had been asking to be transferred, and it just never happened. My request had been fulfilled, but I could not figure out why. In hindsight, I can see that it was God changing my situation for me and introducing me to new friends. I am so very glad now.

In my new department, there was a guy who was always getting picked on. His name was Jason. Jason was a Christian and a very good man. He was always singing uplifting, happy songs about Jesus. In return, all of our coworkers mocked him and picked on him. At times, they were relentless. I fit in more with the crowd that was mocking him, but I began standing up for my new friend. Jason and I began talking more. I felt drawn to him, but I had no idea why.

Jason began telling me about Jesus and sharing Bible verses with me. I had been raised in church, so I knew about God, Jesus, and all the stories that they tell you as a kid in Sunday school. But rebellion ruled my teenage years and taught me to think that I had plenty of time and that I could make myself right with God when I was close to death. So I felt free to do whatever I wanted as a teenager. The things that Jason told me, however, were different than what I was told as a child. I was always taught that God had to be appeased. Jason told me about a God who loved me and sent His Son to die on a cross to pay for my sins. There was something in the way that he told the story that drew me to it. I noticed that I was constantly grabbing my Bible and reading it as if I could not get enough. I craved it so desperately, as if it were food and I had been starving for years.

One day at work, Jason came through the doors singing loudly as usual. The other guys, I remember, were brutally making fun of him on that day. But I noticed the look on Jason's face; he was not hurt or even upset. He just continued singing happily. How could he be happy when others were making fun of him? I yelled at them to shut up and leave Jason alone. They laughed and walked away, and Jason walked over to me. He told me that there was going to be a Christmas play at his church and asked me if I would like to go see it. I graciously accepted.

On the night of the play, I met Jason at the planned spot and then followed him to his church, which was about an hour away. It wasn't until we arrived that I realized that he was actually in the play. We also were very early because Jason had to prepare for the performance. He showed me to the seating area, and I sat down. I was alone in a huge church with nothing but time. All that I could do was think. I hated to be alone, and I hated to just sit and think.

I was very glad when the play started. Not very long into the play, the most amazing thing happened. I was enjoying the play immensely, and somehow I felt as if I were being transported to another dimension. I was still in the same room, and the play was still going on. But like you would see in the movies, I was somehow having a conversation in another world. While the rest of the people in the church watched the play, I had a conversation with God. It was an amazing experience, and I actually heard the audible voice of God speak to me. He asked me if I was done running. He wanted to know if I was ready to turn my entire life back over to Him and believe in His Son to save me from my sins and live for Him from this point on. All I could do was cry hysterically and cry out to God: "Yes! Please forgive me! I can't stand the person I've become. Please take my life and make it whole!" I will never be able to explain what happened that night, but I left a changed person. I felt clean from the inside out, and I felt—dare I say it—happy.

I felt a joy that I could not explain—one that I have never experienced before in my life.

I went home that night a changed person. I cannot explain why, but I just felt differently within. Where there once was nothing but hopelessness, there was now an unexplainable sense of joy and a peace that everything was going to be all right. I decided to start going to a church that my mom had been begging me to try. It seemed fine, and I felt comfortable there. I decided to continue attending and see what happened.

As like before, I had no idea how big the changes that were heading my way were. Amazing things were coming. Things I could have never imagined.

Chapter Four

Take It to the Cross

I had been attending that new church for a little while when the singles pastor asked me to begin coming to the singles' Bible study that he had been leading. The pastor let me know that he would be away the following week but that his friend was going to take over teaching the study for that week and that he would love for me to come. It would be a great chance to meet new friends and learn more about God's word. I was excited to go to the study.

The night of the Bible study, my mom came over to babysit for me. I grabbed my Bible, and I was ready to learn all that God had in store for me. On the way, however, I got nervous. I almost decided not to go. I talked myself into just going shopping instead, but something changed my mind. An inner voice from deep within said this: "Just go!" So even though I was very nervous about showing up, I went.

As I walked into the building, I realized that I was going to be completely embarrassed. I was so eager with my Bible in hand. But I found out that the pastor's friend leading the study had decided to change it to a surprise birthday party for one of the members instead. Of course, I was the only person that was surprised! I was horrified and totally embarrassed. I didn't know a soul there. It was clear that I did not belong there, yet for some reason—most likely pure fear—I stayed. I sat all evening talking to the birthday boy's mother.

What I did not realize was that the man whose birthday we were all celebrating had spent the evening flirting with me. I had no clue that he was even interested.

♦ ♦ ♦

The following Sunday I saw the birthday boy at church. His name was Cary. We talked for a while, and he asked me if I would like to go out on a date with him. I accepted his offer. That weekend on the night before my son's first birthday party, Cary and I went on our first date. There have not been many times since then that we have not been together. Cary even came the next day to my son's birthday party. Cary and my son adored each other.

A few weeks later, Cary asked me to go to a concert with him and another couple that he knew. I had never heard of the performer, and I hadn't been to a concert in many years, so I was so excited—until I walked into the building.

As with any concert, as soon as we walked in, we saw nothing but merchandise for that particular artist. I had no problem with that. I had a problem with the voice inside me pulling me to a T-shirt in the room. In that moment, I felt like the only person in the room, and I was drawn to that stack of T-shirts like in one of those old cartoons. I read the back of the shirt, which had the words to one of the artist's songs on it. It was about an aborted baby praying for his or her mom.

Suddenly, everything I had worked so hard to forget came rushing back into my mind. I remembered the abortion, the child, the regret, the guilt, and the remorse. My mind was flooded with emotion and memories that I swore I would never consider again. Suddenly, I felt like I could not breathe. Somehow, from deep within my soul, I knew that I would not be able to hide this secret guilt of mine any longer. I would no longer be able to forget this part of my life. The pain of that reality was unbelievable.

Cary and I had been dating only for a few weeks, so I reminded myself that I could not fall apart. I had to pull myself together. I could break down after I was home. I shoved it all back down inside me for the very last time and enjoyed the concert—until the last song.

The concert was great, and the singer had the most beautiful voice. I really did enjoy myself, even though every second I had to push down the pain in my throat that reminded me that the artist would sing that song eventually. Then it happened. She told her audience that she had one more song to sing. She stated that it had powerful words about something that was very near and dear to her heart. The piano started playing gently as the artist sat down on the edge of the stage. Softly, she sang the words to this beautiful song. I could hold it in no longer.

Steph Loughman

I remembered my abortion and—more importantly—my child. Tears rolled down my cheeks as I tried desperately to control myself. I could not listen to the words; I could not even move. I tried desperately to get myself up to go to the hallway or the bathroom; I wanted to do anything but sit there and let people see me cry! My family taught me well to never let anyone see me cry, and here I was failing again. I could not make any part of my body move. The tears flowed so heavily that it felt as if there was a river forming at my feet. I could not move my head, but I could see the other couple that we were with sitting up in their seats. They were looking at me. I was sure everyone in that building was looking at me, that they knew what I had done, and that they would look at me as a monster from then on. I was also certain that Cary would never want to see me again.

Somehow, I survived the song, and we left the concert. I honestly do not remember about the ride home. But I do remember that just before we arrived back at my house, Cary and I began to talk. I don't even remember how the conversation got started. I admitted to Cary that I had had an abortion. I had never uttered those words to anyone before. It was not releasing, and it did not feel good to get it out. I was ashamed. I knew full well what I had done. I was well aware that it was not a "fetus" or a "clump of tissues" but that it was my child. I had let my child down and allowed him to be murdered for my own personal safety. That's not a parent. A mother should give her own life for her child. Oh, how I wished I had done that!

I do not recall much about the conversation—except one very important part. I must have mentioned to Cary that I felt so horrible about what I had done. His reply would be something that I would never forget for the rest of my life. He simply told me that if I felt guilty for what I had done, there was no need to worry because Jesus had died for that sin too. All that I had to do was to leave my guilt at the foot of the cross.

When he spoke those words, we were back at my house, sitting out in the driveway in his car. I was shocked. Is that really all that I had to do? How did I do that? All I had ever known was to stuff pain down and that my actions were mostly failures. It was the first time that I realized that Jesus really did die on the cross for every sin that I had committed and that I did not need to hang on to the guilt and shame from it anymore. This was a very new feeling for me, and it would take quite a while for me to understand just how powerful the truth that Cary shared with me was.

I tossed and turned all night long, wondering how I could turn my guilt over to God. I wasn't living two thousand years in the past, nor did I live in the Middle East where Jesus had once lived. How was I supposed to leave something at the foot of the cross? As I considered this and struggled to understand the meaning of that wonderful new phrase, I began singing a song in my mind. It was a song that I had sung in church many times when I was growing up. I could still hear Momaw singing it with a big smile on her face. The song talked about having a heavy heart and telling all of your problems to Jesus. I remembered listening to the words of this song, watching

Momaw's face and thinking of how it seemed like Jesus was her best friend and she was just taking her problems to Him and talking to a good friend.

Was talking to Jesus and taking things to Him really this easy? Could I really tell Jesus something this terrible? Would He still love me anyway? I couldn't yet see that Jesus already knew what I had done; in fact, He knew I would do it before He even created me. Jesus loved me anyway and still went up on that cross for my sin; forgiveness for my sins was already done. All I had to do was accept His forgiveness.

I spent the rest of that night crying and praying. I cried out to God and begged Him for forgiveness. Then the tears streamed down my face when I realized that He had forgiven me and that I could be free from my sin.

Then I asked God to do something else. It was a quick request because I was sure that it was not all right for me to ask this of God, but I desperately needed God to do this. I prayed, "God, if he does not hate me, and if it would be all right, could you please tell my baby that I am so sorry? Please tell him that I love him so very much and that I hope he can find it in his heart to forgive me one day!"

At some point, I cried myself to sleep. After going through so much heartbreak that evening, I finally felt at peace about my future and my happiness. I was going to be all right. I wasn't sure how or why, and I most definitely did not yet feel worthy of God's forgiveness, but God had given me a peace that everything was going to be all right. That was enough for me. Well, I felt peaceful for the time being anyway.

Chapter Five

A Wonderful Dream

Things went well for Cary and me, and we got married that summer. He adopted my son, and we had more kids of our own as well. Things were shaping us to make us a nice little family. However, even though I was so blessed, I felt an overwhelming sadness at times. Though I tried desperately, I could not shake this sadness. I couldn't even explain what it was or where it had come from.

There was one night in particular when I felt as if I could not go on anymore. I felt so bad for feeling this way because I had a loving husband and my precious babies. I adored every second that I had with my family, but I could not explain my sadness. When Cary came home from work that night, he could tell by looking at me that I could not take another second. He gave me a hug, told me that he loved me, and then told me that he wanted me to go straight to bed. He wanted me to spend some time crying out to God and asking God to show me why I was so devastated.

That is exactly what I did. As I sat on our bed, I cried out to God. I asked Him to show me what was going on inside my head. I asked God how I could be so miserable when I had so many wonderful things in my life and how I could overcome my misery and begin living again. All of these questions weighed so heavily on my mind. I cried so hard. I must have exhausted myself, and at some point, I fell asleep.

I must have cried even more than I could have imagined because even in my dream, I was crying. And my tears and sobbing had become uncontrollable. I was at one of my favorite places on earth—the beach. I wondered how I could be in such a wonderful place and still be so sad. I absolutely loved hearing the sound of the water crashing onto the shore, the smell of the salty air, and the feel of the cool ocean breeze on my face. But suddenly, I understood why I was crying. I was mourning the child that I had aborted.

It was true that I had given my pain to Jesus, asked for His forgiveness, and left my sin at the cross, but I had yet to deal with the fact that I was a mother to a dead child. I hadn't yet grieved the loss of that precious young life. Somehow, from somewhere deep within me, I knew that it was the time to do that.

I felt the wonderful warm ocean breeze on my face. I heard the waves crash onto the shore just a few steps away from where I sat. But all that I could do was weep, and I wept hysterically.

As I was trying to settle down, I felt the presence of another person. I looked up and saw a child staring at me. I felt a strange tug on my heart as I looked at this beautiful child. I had a feeling that I knew who he was, but I thought it was not possible that he was my child. My child was dead because

The Journey

I had allowed a doctor to abort my precious little one long before it was time for him to be born. This could not possibly be my baby. But he looked so much like his siblings. It had to be him!

This had to be my child, but I thought that he would not want to see me! Surely, he knew that I gave the permission for his murder. He certainly would not want to see me. I wanted to get away from there. I wanted to run to him and hug him so badly, but I thought he surely hated me. My mind was running at a thousand miles a minute. Then I noticed he was running toward me. I thought to myself, "No!" I turned away; I could not face him.

My child stopped running right before he got to me. He confirmed that he was indeed my son Joshua. I turned away from him and sobbed even more loudly. How could this be? I didn't deserve to see him, and I wondered how I could ever apologize to him. I had no right to tell him how much I had missed him and how much I loved him. I could not believe that this was even happening!

My sobbing had become very uncontrollable at that point, and I seemed to be shaking hysterically. My child moved in close to me and put his precious little hand on my shoulder. Oh, how I had wished for that day! However, my crying became even worse. I could not stop; I had absolutely no control anymore. Then the most amazing thing that I will never forget happened.

My precious child—the same one whom I aborted and whom I had no right to even so much as be around—wrapped his arms around me in the most loving way I've ever imagined. I had killed this child, yet he still loved me deeply. All that I could do was cry. Then I cried more and then some more. All the while, my son held me in his arms. He just loved me—all he ever wanted was to love me.

The tears I cried that day were beyond healing. I cannot even describe the feeling that came from that good long cry. What followed was even more healing. My son, whom I had named Joshua, and I just sat and talked. He told me that he was happy living in heaven and that he wanted me to be happy. He even told me stories about our family members who were in heaven with him. One of his best friends was Momaw! Oh, how I've missed her! It was so comforting to know that they were so close.

Joshua and I talked as we sat in the sand. We talked more as we walked along the shore. It was such a wonderful and healing time. Joshua told me that Jesus had told him how sad I had been and that neither Jesus nor Joshua wanted me to be sad. He desperately wanted me to be happy and live my life. Then Joshua told me that one day I would go to heaven and be with him, Momaw, and Jesus. This precious little man had been through so much, and his only concern was for me.

I told my son about his siblings. I also told him about Cary and let him know that Cary was his daddy. When Cary adopted my older son, he adopted Joshua as well and loved him as if he was his own. I let Joshua know that after his daddy had adopted him, the two of us decided to have a memorial service for Joshua, and that it was then that he was given his name, Joshua. My beautiful son and I talked about how special he was and how much his family loved him.

I enjoyed a very special time with Joshua. We talked and spent time together. I cried more, but the tears were different. The remorse was gone. There was no more guilt and shame. There was only love for my precious child. I would remember that night for the rest of my life and hold it close to my heart.

We watched the sun go down, and we knew our time was almost over. I thanked Joshua for coming to see me and told him that I loved him very much. I told him not to worry. I told him that I would try to be happier in my life for him and that I could not wait to join him in heaven. We hugged, and it was so wonderful. Then he was gone.

As I sat on the beach alone again, I felt at peace. I had not only mourned the loss of my son, but I had had the opportunity to tell him how much I loved him and missed him. I knew that he did not hate me. He loved me just as dearly as I loved him. I sat on the shore enjoying the water as it made its way past my toes. I dug my feet in the sand and felt the cool ocean breeze hit my face and dry my tears. I thanked God for giving me such a wonderful experience. I noticed that my eyelids were getting heavier and heavier. This was a dream for sure, and it was ending. But I felt different. I wasn't sure exactly how I felt different, but I knew that my life would be different from then on.

I wondered what Joshua was doing back in heaven. I hoped that he told his Momaw hi for me and let her know how much I missed her.

Chapter Six

Friends and Forgiveness

I woke up in a puddle of my own tears. As I rubbed my eyes, I tried to focus on reality. That had to have been just a dream. It couldn't have been real—could it? Had I really just met my child? Did he really still love me even though I was to blame for his death? It was all so amazing. I just wasn't sure what to think; my head was spinning.

As I became fully awake and began getting myself ready for the day, I found myself constantly going back to that wonderful dream. I would smile and giggle to myself when I remembered spending time with my son—what an amazing young man he was! I wondered if I should tell others about what had happened or if I should keep the treasure of meeting him to myself and hide it deep in my heart. I wasn't sure of the right answer, but I had to get going and begin my day.

♦ ♦ ♦

I had a busy day planned—homeschooling my children; going to the grocery store, which always took forever with six little ones in tow because people always stared and asked if all six children were mine; getting some lesson plans done; and maybe even trying to get a few minutes to myself to breathe. However, all of my plans came to a halt when my phone rang.

On the other end of the phone was my pastor. He had talked to a lady earlier that day and thought that I might be the better person to help her with her problem. This young lady, whose name was Kayleigh, was struggling with life; she didn't feel that she had the will or the right to live anymore. She felt this way because she was suffering severe guilt and shame over having an abortion.

My pastor knew of my struggles because I had talked privately with him, but I had also gone in front of my church and asked for prayer. I had shared my testimony. Since that night at the concert with Cary, I had gone through so much and learned so much about forgiveness. I knew that Jesus had forgiven me for my sin and that He loved me anyway. I found grace and forgiveness in Jesus; after I spoke to my son, I finally began to forgive myself. Suddenly, my pastor—and surely my God too—was asking me to share forgiveness with a young lady who had reached out to him.

I told my pastor that I would be glad to talk to Kayleigh and took down her phone number. He let me know that she would not be available to talk until later on that afternoon. So I went about homeschooling and getting my grocery shopping done. I decided to call her while the kids were napping.

Steph Loughman

I was anxious that whole afternoon about talking to Kayleigh. I was excited to be given the chance to help another person, but I realized the intense responsibility of the situation as well. This woman was going to depend on me for finding hope in life again. I remember thinking this: "What if I say something wrong? What will happen if I mess this up in some way? Would she slip further into depression? Oh, this is not good!" I suddenly realized that I was not capable of helping this woman!

Later that day, as I considered all of this, I realized that I had gotten myself very upset. I was ready to call my pastor back and tell him that there was no way that I could to talk to Kayleigh because I did not want to mess her up even more. As I thought about calling my pastor, I thought of what he would say to me. The very first thing that went through my mind was a Bible story from the book of Exodus. It was the story of Moses and of how God wanted Moses to speak to Pharaoh. Moses came up with every excuse he could, just as I was doing now, and God had an answer for each excuse.

I remembered a verse I had just taught my kids, Deuteronomy 31:6, which says, "Be strong and courageous. Do not be afraid or terrified because of them, for the Lord your God goes with you; he will never leave you nor forsake you." Wow, how could I be afraid to talk to Kayleigh after reciting this verse? But I still was.

I knew God had brought that verse to my mind and that He was reminding me that He was in control. He did not want me to worry but to trust Him. I pulled out my Bible; I was going to need some more verses of encouragement.

I went to the book of Isaiah—always a great source of encouragement and a reminder that God is with me always. Chapter 41 had two verses that stuck out to me. Isaiah 41:10 says, "So do not fear, for I am with you; do not be dismayed, for I am your God. I will strengthen you and help you; I will uphold you with my righteous right hand." Isaiah 41:13 says, "For I am the Lord your God who takes hold of your right hand and says to you, 'do not fear; I will help you.'"

I love how God speaks to me through His word. There was no need for me to be afraid. He already had me covered, and He would guide me as I talked to Kayleigh. She was His child, after all, and since my goal was to point her to Him and His forgiveness, the job was actually God's job. He would simply use me to bring Kayleigh to Him. I felt honored that God would use me to help others.

With my mind set back on God and His purpose, I was finally ready to call Kayleigh. Before I did though, I did one more thing. Since I was doing God's work, I felt that I needed to take a minute to pray.

I prayed these words: "Precious Jesus, I thank You for this opportunity. I am so glad that You would use me, and in doing so, You can take something as horrible as abortion and use it for good to help other people. Lord, please bless this conversation. Help Kayleigh to receive the words that You give me to speak, and let her find Your amazing grace and forgiveness. Help her to know, just as You have shown me, that her child is in heaven with You and that Your desire is for her to be happy and to trust in You. Father, please open Kayleigh's heart to You and help her to experience the freedom that can only be found in Your love. I love You so much, and I praise You for all that You have given us. I ask all of this in Your most precious name. Amen."

Earlier that morning, I had felt fear. I had felt unprepared for the strong spiritual battle that I was about to face. After spending time in God's word and in prayer, I felt fully prepared and equipped; I felt ready to begin using my abortion for God's glory.

The phone seemed to ring forever before Kayleigh answered. She later admitted that she knew that I was calling and that she was nervous to talk to me. I was just ready to hang up when she answered. I could tell that she was scared and wasn't sure if she wanted this conversation to happen or not. I decided to begin by telling my new friend about myself to take the pressure off of her.

I told Kayleigh about my past without making it a drawn-out story. After giving her enough information about my past to explain my present, I went into the story of my abortion. I told her that I loved my child and had planned on keeping him but that I got scared and made the decision very quickly.

I explained to Kayleigh that I was pretty far along in my pregnancy when I had the abortion. I was seventeen weeks, which was long enough to feel the baby grow inside me, to watch my stomach grow, and to feel him moving inside of me. I already felt very close with my precious little one before that one horrible morning when I quickly decided that it all should end.

Then I told my new friend about the concert and that beautiful song that spoke so strongly to me. I went on to explain about how God drew things out in me that I didn't even realize I was struggling with because of the abortion. Not only did God make me think about and deal with these things, but in the end, He also showed me grace and forgiveness.

It amazed me every time I looked back at the whole thing. God not only pulled me out of my misery, but He also gave me hope—more hope than I've ever known in my life. I came to the point where I realized that there was life after an abortion and that life could still be good. This is what I wanted Kayleigh to understand. I asked her if she was willing to do the very hard work of bringing her horror out so that she could feel better about herself. I told her that it would be like pouring peroxide on an open wound. Dealing with her abortion was going to sting. It was going to burn and hurt, but in the end, everything would be cleaned out and better. Dealing with this would enable her to be able to live with herself again.

Kayleigh was in tears. She would sob, then go quiet, and then sob again. Every once in a while, I would hear her whisper, "Yes...Yes," as if in agreement with what I was telling her. Other than that, she was very quiet. It broke my heart to know that she was hurting so badly; I knew the pain that she felt very personally. On the other hand, however, I was excited to know that she was stepping onto the road to recovery and that God was going to use me to show her the freedom of forgiveness.

I asked Kayleigh if she would like to join me in a group that met to talk through past abortions and to lift each other up in prayer and encouragement. She said that she would very much like to do that. We also agreed to meet weekly with just the two of us in order to do a Bible study and help each other. We were going to be very good friends. I could tell that for sure.

I wanted to talk to Kayleigh about one more thing. There was something that she could do to begin her healing, and I wanted her to go ahead and begin to think of this so that she could get started on her healing as soon as possible. Kayleigh was eager to begin healing, and she asked what it was that I wanted her to do. I told her that she needed to commemorate her child, acknowledge that this life was her son or daughter, and begin to mourn that loss. She agreed that this needed to be done and asked me how to do this.

Abortion causes the death of a child, but it is different in a way because the mother normally has no way of knowing the sex of the baby. In order to fully recognize that the aborted child was a human life, it is important for the mother to spend some time in prayer, asking God to show her whether the baby was a boy or a girl, and to name the child.

Kayleigh quickly informed me that she did not have to spend any time in prayer on this because she already had been doing so. She was sure that God had shown her that her child was a girl and that He told her that the child's name was Sierra.

I thought that it was so awesome that she had already taken this step in her healing, and I thought Sierra was such a beautiful name. I told Kayleigh that God was going to do amazing things through her and that I was very excited to see what God was going to do through the both of us. We had only just met, and we both had very long and hard roads to walk, but I was willing to walk with my new friend. I could just tell that we were going to become the very best of friends. I became so excited.

Chapter Seven

A Purpose for Joshua and Sierra

In the months that followed, Kayleigh and I became very close friends. We held each other up in the hard times, and we laughed together through the good times. We spent time together often, and we talked at least once daily. I was saddened by the circumstances that brought us together as friends, but at the same time, I praised God for the good friend that He had given me in her. We even joked often about how we were sure that Joshua and Sierra were best friends in heaven and were waiting for us to join them.

After spending time in prayer, Kayleigh and I both thought that God was calling us to begin a ministry in honor of our children. Cary was very supportive of this, and Tracy, Kayleigh's fiancé, was also supportive. Both Cary and Tracy were godly men and always supported us in whatever we did. Cary and Tracy grew up together, so they knew each other very well and always stood behind Kayleigh and me on our ventures.

One night, the four of us went to dinner to discuss our new ministry. We were going to be a team in this, so we wanted to be certain that we did it right. To do it correctly, the very first thing that we needed to do was pray. We all had been praying individually for quite some time, but we knew that it was time to come together and bring this to God as the team that we had become. As we sat in our corner booth in that restaurant praying for God's guidance, I could feel the Holy Spirit wrap around us so intensely that I felt as if I could cry. This truly was going to be something amazing!

The ministry was going to be for men and women who had experienced an abortion. We wanted to show others that there was hope for them and that they still could be forgiven and loved. Cary and Tracy would even help as they would be able to offer hope to men who had encountered abortion so these men would also know that the things that they were feeling were normal as well. Cary had been with me since the beginning of my healing, and he had adopted Joshua. He knew firsthand how it felt to be with a woman who had had an abortion, and he could help men with the many emotions about the things that had happened to their mates. Tracy had helped his girlfriend get an abortion in high school, so he also knew very well the guilt and shame that came from being involved with the decision to abort a child and would be able to help men struggling with guilt. This ministry was going to be such a great blessing and very much needed.

After a woman has an abortion, she is supposed to just go back to normal life and forget everything that happened. But that is simply not possible. Someone has to stand up and speak for these women so that they know that it is OK to come out of hiding. We had an important message for these women: they could have a life and be happy again! There was a way to let go of all the guilt, shame, and remorse of having an abortion. We knew that the only way out was Jesus. He forgives, loves, and helps us move on. I shivered at the thought of being able to use my story to help other people. The ministry would give purpose to Joshua and Sierra's short and very precious lives. I hoped they would somehow see and be happy about what we were doing.

◆ ◆ ◆

After a few months, things were progressing quite well. Kayleigh and I had started a Bible study on the aftereffects of abortion, and a few ladies were participating in the group. These precious women were beginning to see hope in their lives. They had begun praying and asking God to show them the sex of their children so that they could name them and memorialize them, which was such a wonderful thing to witness.

However, I had not been feeling well, and because of Cary and Kayleigh's pushing, I had made a doctor's appointment. I was pregnant and had recently found out that I was having twins. While I was very excited, something from deep within me made me too afraid to be excited. It was as if I knew what I was going to find out at that appointment.

I was not surprised when my doctor told me that I needed to rush over to the women's center to have an emergency ultrasound. I do not know how, but somewhere deep down,

The Journey

I knew what was happening. I tried to prepare myself for the inevitable news that the ultrasound confirmed. I called Cary to have him join me. Earlier that day, I had told him to go to work and that I would be OK, but I thought he would want to be there for the ultrasound.

As we walked back into the little room with the ultrasound machine, I looked at my husband, and my heart broke. I hadn't told him about my fears, but I could see them written all over his face. I could not speak. That must not have been a problem only for me because as soon as the ultrasound pictures came up on the screen, the room fell silent. The ultrasound technician excused herself and said that she needed to get a doctor before she could go any further.

The look on the doctor's face was all that I needed to know the truth. The only words that I could get out were these: "Will either of the babies make it?" He shook his head and explained that both of my babies were already gone. The broken pieces that were left of my heart shattered even more.

I was taken to the hospital where I had to deliver my babies and be treated myself so that I would recover physically. Cary and I got to hold our tiny babies before the nurse took both of them so that the doctor could try and find out what went wrong. I cherished the time that we held our tiny ones and told them that we loved them so very much. I so wished that we could have more time with them. Other than those sweet words, Cary and I did not talk; there were no words to say. Tracy and Kayleigh visited us and prayed with us. It was so good to have them there.

After I recovered physically from losing my twins, I realized that I still had a huge emotional struggle. It took some help, but I realized that I blamed myself for the miscarriage. Even though I had carried other babies to full term, I had convinced myself that if I had not had the abortion, the twins wouldn't have died. Kayleigh was so wonderful in talking to me and helping me realize that this was a lie from Satan. She reminded me that I needed to memorialize my children, just like I had told her that she needed to memorialize Sierra.

I discussed memorializing our babies with Cary, and we agreed that it was very important. We knew that there was one boy and one girl, which made it easier to name them. We decided to name our daughter Lissa, and our son was named Brett. My heart was so very broken, but I felt it beginning to heal.

The memorial service was beautiful and helped tremendously in the healing process. Cary and I stood with our children, and a very dear friend sang a beautiful song in memory of our children. We looked at the ultrasound pictures that we had saved and at pictures that we had taken the day that they were born. We had a picture of each of our living children holding the babies and a family picture with all of us. It was a very precious time.

That evening, I walked into my bedroom and fell on my bed. I allowed myself the release of tears, and I clung to the pictures of the twins in my mind. I thought of Brett and Lissa running around in heaven with Joshua. I was sure that they would be close and would enjoy each other's company. How happy they must be about getting to know each other. I imagined them sitting at the feet of Jesus, and Jesus telling them how much He loved them. I was sure that Momaw was giving them all kinds of love too. I knew that I would hold those images in my heart until the day that I died.

My precious children came into my bedroom that night, and one by one, they told me how much they loved me and gave me kisses on the cheek and soft hugs. After tucking them into their beds for the night, Cary wrapped his arms around me, and we cried together. I fell asleep with beautiful images of my beautiful children in my mind—images of my living children playing in heaven with the ones who had passed. Cary and I watched and smiled. What a beautiful family I had been blessed with. I thought about what a beautiful day it would be when we would all be united in heaven. I knew that I would hold on to that night and the images in my mind until the day I died.

I now know that the day will soon come for me to walk through those glorious gates and see Jesus; I'm certain that He will allow my children to be first in line to welcome me and usher me into His glory. I know that will be a day of great rejoicing!

A Message for You

If you are struggling with the effects of a past abortion, it is important for you to know that you are not alone. There are many men and women who have come forward and embraced the grace, mercy, and forgiveness that Jesus so freely offers. This very same Jesus is holding out His loving arms for you right this moment. Your child is in heaven with Him and has nothing but love for you.

The many emotions that you are dealing with are completely normal and are felt by most women who have had an abortion. There are countless men and women attempting to hide the pain deep within them for fear of others judging them for what they have done. It is important to understand that hiding your pain is a tool Satan uses to keep you bound by your pain.

I strongly encourage you to break free from these chains and reach out to a person that can help you deal with this pain so that you are able to forgive yourself and remember how good life can be. Seek out a pastor or a friend. Or you can visit a local Crisis Pregnancy Center. You can also find more information at www.facebook.com/TheJourneyStephLoughman. You are welcome to message me directly on that page, and I will gladly stand in the gap and pray for you. I have firsthand knowledge of the pain caused by abortion and would be very happy to help you find peace and forgiveness through Jesus Christ. I look forward to hearing from you.

Made in the USA
Middletown, DE
08 June 2016